COMPUTER EDUCATION I

Grade 7 Module

QUILINGUIN

NEUST - Gabaldon

Author: **ALDRIN DAVE S. QUILINGUIN**
	Faculty of Nueva Ecija University of Science and Technology - Gabaldon Campus, College of Information and Communication Technology.

Editor: **Andie T. Capinding**
	Faculty of Nueva Ecija University of Science and Technology - Gabaldon Campus, College of Education.

COMPUTER EDUCATION 1
ALDRIN DAVE S. QUILINGUIN

Module 1 - COMPUTER SYSTEM

Overview:

This module is primarily designed to equip the student with an adequate knowledge necessary to the understanding and appreciation of computers as data processing tools. It aims to provide adequate computer literacy to students who are only beginning to earn and understand the highly technical field of computer science. The prepared course of study is ideally suited for teaching those who have no previous knowledge of and exposure to computers.

It is believed that once a fundamental understanding is attained, the students will be in a better position to start exploring the depths and wonders of computers and its related technology.

For many of us, a computer is just known as a piece of equipment – that awesome package of glass, plastic, metal and wires – used to make our work easier. It is now possible for us to see the world in a different way, to achieve new goals, which were impossible before, and to control the world around us. Computers have actually transformed our lives – how we communicate, how we work and learn things and even how we play. Computers are efficient tools in processing data into useful information.

These are essential tools in almost every field of research and applied technology because of their capabilities. And because of the widespread use and availability of computers, it is essential that everyone acquires an understanding of what computers are and how they work. In the modern world, no one can afford to be ignorant of the important role of computers in any career or business of choice. Being computer literate will give anyone a great competitive advantage.

LESSON 1: COMPUTER SYSTEM

Computer – is an electronic device which consists of several components that together provide the capability of executing a stored program. It is a device that accepts data, processes and stores these, and produces output. It performs four basic functions such as input, process, storage and output.

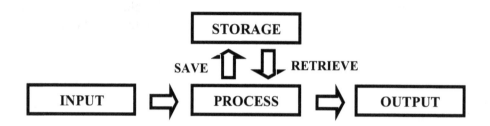

Basic Computer Functions

A computer system has three main elements: mainly, the *hardware*, *software* and the most important, the *Information Technology (IT) professionals or peopleware*. These three elements interact with one another in order to produce desired information from a given set of data.

LESSON 1.1: ELEMENTS OF A COMPUTER SYSTEM

A. **HARDWARE** – refers to the physical components of the computer system that you can   actually touch.
    -   tangible parts of the computer.
    Examples:
        keyboard, monitor, speaker, mouse and Central Processing Unit (CPU)

B. **SOFTWARE** – it is a set of instructions or programs that tells the computer what to do a specific task. These are the programs used by the user to interact with the computer.
    - intangible parts of the computer.
    Examples:
        MS Word, MS Excel, MS Power Point and Encarta

C. PEOPLEWARE – the people who use the computer system. They are the most important factor in a computer system because they manipulate and program the computer system to make it useful.

> \- skilled person in Information Technology (IT).

Examples:
> Programmer, System Analyst, Data Encoder and Computer Librarian

A. HARDWARE

Hardware may be classified into *Input Devices*, *Output Devices*, *Central Processing Unit (CPU)* and *Secondary Storage*.

1. INPUT DEVICE – consists of external devices that provides information and instructions to the computer.

Different Input Devices

a. Keyboard – it is use for entering characters.

Parts:

Alphanumeric Keys	Special Keys	Numeric Keys
Functions Keys	Arrow Keys	

b. Mouse – a pointing device that used to move the pointer on the screen.

Parts:

Wire or Cord	Right Click Button
Left Click Button	Wheel or Scroll
Palm Rest	

Kinds:

- *Mechanical Mouse* – it is a computer mouse that contains a metal or rubber ball on its underside. When the ball is rolled in any directions, sensors inside the mouse detect this motion and move the on-screen mouse pointer in the same direction.

- *Optical Mouse* – it is a computer mouse which uses a light source, typically a light-emitting diode, and a light detector, such as an array of photodiodes, to detect movement relative to a surface.

- *Wireless Mouse* – a mouse that send signals to the computer without a cord.

c. Trackball – a pointing device similar to a mouse but the ball on top is the one directly moved the pointer on the screen.

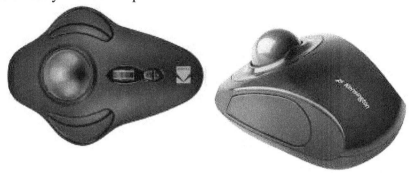

d. Joystick – a pointing device with a base and a vertical handle that pivots in all directions.

e. Touch Screen – a display screen that allows users to interact with the system by touching specific areas on the screen.

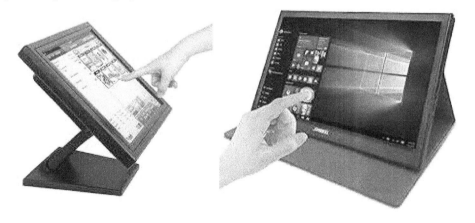

f. Light Pen – it is a sensitive stylus or pen device that is used by engineers, illustrators and graphic designers.

g. Graphics Tablet – it is sometimes called digitizing tablet that connected by a wire to a light pen through which the user can sketch images.

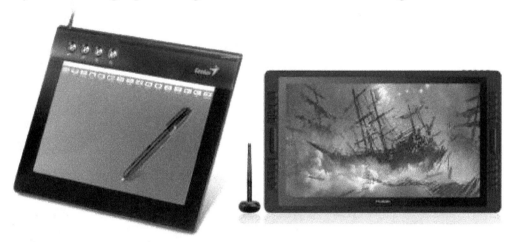

h. Scanning Device – translates image of text, photo and other graphics into digital form.

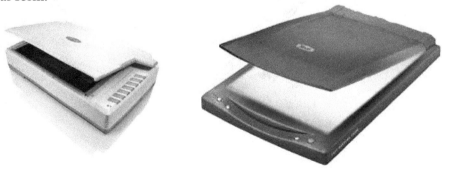

i. **Bar Code Reader** – a handheld scanner that translates bar code symbols into digital forms.

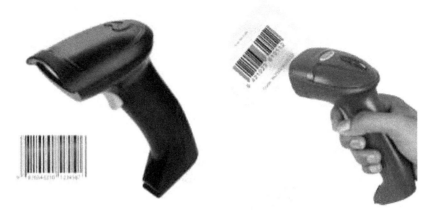

j. **Fax Machine or Facsimile Transmission Machine** – scans hardcopy and transmits data to another fax machine using telephone lines.

k. **Magnetic Stripe Card** – contains data encoded and stored on magnetic stripes.

l. Multimedia Devices – record music and other sound signals and transform them into digital format to be used as inputs for PCs.

m. Digital Cameras – capture images in electronic form for immediate viewing on a computer screen.

2. **OUTPUT DEVICE** – consists of devices which communicate the result of processing back to the user.

Different Output Devices

a. **Monitor** – displays images using grids of dots called pixels.
    -   it produces soft copy.

Kinds:

1. Cathode Ray Tube (CRT) – kinds of monitor that looks like traditional TV set.

2. Flat Panel Display

Kinds:

- Liquid Crystal Display (LCD) – it is a flat-panel display or other electronically modulated optical device that uses the light-modulating properties of liquid crystals combined with polarizers. Liquid crystals do not emit light directly, instead using a backlight or reflector to produce images in color or monochrome.

- Plasma Display – it is a computer video display in which each pixel on the screen is illuminated by a tiny bit of plasma or charged gas, somewhat like a tiny neon light.

- Light Emitting Diode (LED) – a flat-panel display that uses an array of light-emitting diodes as pixels for a video display. Their brightness allows them to be used outdoors where they are visible in the sun for store signs and billboards.

b. **Printer** – used to output information shown on the screen on a printed paper.
   - it produces hard copy

Categories:

- Impact printer – refers to a class of printers that work by hanging a head or needle against an ink ribbon to make a mark on the paper

Example:

⇒ *Dot Matrix Printer (DMP)* – is a type of printer which uses pins impacting an ink ribbon to print.

- Non-impact printer – a type of printer that does not operate by striking a head against a ribbon.

Examples:

⇒ Laser Printer – it is a popular type of personal computer printer that uses a non-impact (keys don't strike the paper), photocopier technology. When a document is sent to the printer, a laser beam "draws" the document on a selenium-coated drum using electrical charges.

⇒ Inkjet Printer – it is a type computer printing that recreates a digital image by propelling droplets of ink onto paper and plastic substrates.

c. **Speaker** – produces sound output.

d. **Projector** – or image projector is an optical device that projects an image (or moving images) onto a surface, commonly a projector screen.

3. **CENTRAL PROCESSING UNIT (CPU)** – this is the place where the processing and conversion of data from input to output is done. It is also the heart and brain of the computer

4. <u>**SECONDARY STORAGE**</u> – is where the data stored permanently.

A. SOFTWARE

Software may be categorized as *System Software* or *Application Software*.

1. <u>**SYSTEM SOFTWARE**</u> – performs tasks necessary to the efficient management of the hardware. It refers to computer programs or library files whose purpose is to help run the computer system.

   Example:
   Operating Systems

Utility Programs
Compilers and Interpreters

2. **<u>APPLICATION SOFTWARE</u>** – programs that help solve and meet user problems and needs directly. They are designed to perform specific functions, which make daily activities easier and facilitate the performance of work efficiently and effectively.

Example:

MS Word	Photoshop
MS Excel	Internet Explorer
MS PowerPoint	Messenger
Outlook	Youtube
Facebook	AutoCAD

C. PEOPLEWARE

The major compositions of these IT professionals are the management group, systems and procedures group, programming group and the computer operations group. It is a skilled person in the field on Information Technology.

Lesson 2: CLASSIFICATIONS OF COMPUTERS

Today, computers come in different sizes, and shapes, and with unlimited computing capabilities. Because of the rapid development in hardware and software, and the changing needs of the users, we find big and bulky mainframe computers and cute handheld palmtops.

Computers may be classified into the following: according to capacity, with their ability to perform a task, as well as the maximum number of programs they can run; according to purpose, their goals and aims for a variety of tasks; and according to the type of processing, which are their special uses in different fields of work.

Classifications of Computers According to Purpose

According to Purpose	General Purpose Computer	Special Purpose Computer
Application	Handle variety of tasks	Dedicated to a specific task
Advantage	Versatile	• More efficient because of specialized programs • Faster processing
Disadvantage	• Less efficient • Slower	Used only for specific task
Examples	• Personal Computer • PDA	• Play Station • Word processor

Classifications of Computers According to Types of Processing

Analog	Digital	Hybrid
Machines that represent variables or qualities using physical analogies	• Machines that specialize in counting • Use discrete numbers • Result obtained is precise and repeatable	Machines that incorporate measuring capabilities of the analog devices and the counting capability of the digital devices.

Examples:
    Speedometer
    Clock
    Thermometer
	Examples:
	    Digital Clock
	    Digital Thermometer
	    Calculator
		Examples:
		    Ana-Digi Watches
		 (watches with both analog and digital functions)

Classifications of Computers According to Capacity

According To Capacity	Micro-computer	Mini-computer	Main Frame Computer	Super Computer
Other names	Personal Computer	Midrange Computer	Large Scale Computer	
Common Application/Use	• Used in homes, offices • For individual and corporate uses	• For companies needing storage and processing requirements • For more computer power	• For medium to large size business • Used by business and government to provide centralized storage processing and management of data of large amount	• Used to compute intensive tasks • Designed for large-scale complex scientific applications
No. of Users	• Single users • Usually stand-alone to other computers but generally used to carry out processing for a single user	Multiple users, less than 100 users	Multiple users greater than or 100 users	Multiple users
Price Range	₱ 25, 000 – ₱ 250, 000	₱ 250,000 – ₱ 10 Million	₱ 10 Million- ₱ 50 Million	₱ 10 Million – ₱ 2.5 Billion
Speed Processor	5-20 MIPS	25 – 100 MPS	• 440 – 4,500 MIPS • May have several	• 4 – 10 times faster than mainframes

				processors	• Several processors • 60 Billion – 3 Trillion MIPS • Fastest, most processing power
Storage Capacity	32 Mb – 256 Mb of primary storage	32 Mb – 512 Mb of primary storage	50 Mb – several gigabytes of primary storage	8,000 Mb++	
Other Considerations (e.g., space)	• No unusual power required or environment considerations • May fit on top of a table or desk	• Requires controlled environment • Occupies own floor space, like the size of a file cabinet	• Requires controlled environment • Requires full time operators • Housed in a cabinet where peripherals are in separate cabinets	• Requires controlled environment • Space needed may be the size of a car	
Examples	Desktop, notebook, laptop, palmtop, personal digital assistant (PDA)	Network servers, web servers, multiple use systems	Enterprise systems, transaction processors, super server	Scalable servers, Cray Computer, IBM Deep Blue Super Computer	

Lesson 3: GENERATIONS OF COMPUTERS

Generations of the Computer

Fourth-generation computers represent the state of the art today and the fifth generation is on the way. The term "generation" in this context refers to major developments in electronic data processing. In the computer industry, the word "generation" is used as a term of general characterization rather than absolute distinction. These generations are:

1)   First Generation Computers
2)   Second Generation Computers
3)   Third Generation Computers
4)   Fourth Generation Computers

First Generation Computers (1951-1959)

With the beginning of the Korean War in 1950, the demand for many different kinds of computation increased greatly. The appearance of the first commercial computer, the UNIVAC, in 1951, marked the beginning of computers belonging to the first generation. The major innovations then were the use of vacuum tubes in place of relays as a means of storing data in memory and the use of the stored-program concept. The addition of memory made the punched card system and the calculators virtually obsolete. The wire board was replaced by computer programs written in a new language for processing.

Although the vacuum tube was the device that made computers so much faster and more powerful than any of its early predecessors, it had several faults. First of all, it was not a long-0lieve component. The average time between tube failures was 12 hours. It required some 3,500 kilowatts of electricity per day to provide the heat needed to get electrons moving in all of its tubes. Vacuum tubes produced a large amount of heat that computers required air conditioning and special insulation of the tubes to protect the other machine components. Also, the vacuum tube made it necessary to construct enormous and bulky machines.

No educational programs precisely met the requirements of the technology when the first generation computer became available. Early users were pioneering in the use of a new tool not designed specifically for their particular needs. Computer installations had to be staffed with a new breed of workers who initially had to cope with the necessity of preparing programs in a tedious machine language. They were the programmers, the computer operators, and the system analysts. Despite of these obstacles, the computer was found to be a fast, accurate, and untiring tool which man badly needed.

Second Generation Computers (1959-1964)

Solid-state components (transistors and diodes) and magnetic core storage formed the basis for the second generation of computers. The new transistor technology made the previous generation obsolete. A transistor performs the same functions as a vacuum tube, except that electrons move through solid materials instead of through a vacuum. In this period, computers became much smaller in size, faster, more reliable, and much greater I processing capacity. Built-in error detecting devices were installed and more efficient means were developed to input data into and retrieve data from the computer. Also, more efficient programming methods became available.

Essential accessories such as high-speed card readers and printers were being developed. The microsecond was becoming the standard unit for measuring a computer's access to data and instructions. In programming, different languages began to replace machine language. Some companies were starting to build super-computers for scientific research financed by the U.S. government.

Third Generation Computers (1965-1970)

Integrated solid-state circuitry, improved storage devices, and new input/output devices were the most important advances in this generation. The new circuitry increased the speed of the computer by a factor of about 10,000 over the first generation computers. Arithmetic and logical operations were now being performed in microseconds or even nanoseconds. There were related developments that followed. Because of the faster speed of operation, more than one program could be run through the computer at the same time. The smaller size chips improved the computing power and storage capacity of computers. A significant contribution was the remote terminal to permit geographically dispersed users to communicate with a central computer. Unlike the batch processing computer that handled one application at a time, the third generation computer handled many programs and responded to inquires without delay. The on-line, real-time computer mode became a routine environment with most large computers.

IBM ushered in the third generation of computing hardware when it announced its System/360 family of computers in the mid-sixties. There began a trend toward standardization and the IBM 360 was intended to standardize a number of computer characteristics, including instruction codes, units of information and arithmetic modes. Machines continued the trend toward miniaturization of circuit components. Further improvements in speed, cost, and storage capacity were realized.

Fourth Generation Computers (1965-1970)

The major innovations were in the development of microelectronics and in the development of different areas in computer technology such as: multiprocessing, multiprogramming, miniaturization, time-sharing, operation speed, and virtual storage. Because of microprocessors, the fourth generation includes large computers that are much faster, much less expensive, and of much greater data processing capacity than equivalent-sized third generation computers. Also, inexpensive minicomputers and microcomputers proliferated. Among the advanced input/output devices employed in fourth-generation computers are optical readers, audio response terminals, and graphic display terminals.

Lesson 4: CAPABILITIES, LIMITATIONS AND CHARACTERISTICS OF COMPUTERS

As computers developed, they have become more and more a part of our everyday lives. These developments have made significant changes in many people's lives. Computers have edged their way into our lifestyle because of the reduction in size, increase in power or capability and reduction in cost. Having discovered the powerful capabilities of computers, people started to search for practical uses for them. Computers provide new ways of performing old tasks and often called convenience tools

Capabilities

1) They can do repetitive and routine works.
2) They have the speed to process voluminous amount of data in a flash.
3) Computers are reliable and accurate.
4) They can sore and recall tremendous amount of information.
5) Computers have a self-checking ability.
6) Computers can be self-operating.
7) They can do remote processing.

Limitations

1) Computers are always dependent on instructions and data through the program made by the programmer.
2) Computers can never generate information on their own.
3) Computers can never correct wrong instructions.
4) Computers cannot decide if they were not programmed for certain specific tasks.
5) Computers are vulnerable to a virus attack.

Characteristics

1) Speed	5) Versatility
2) Accuracy	6) Reliability
3) Diligence	7) Memory Capability
4) Storage	

Lesson 5: HISTORY OF COMPUTER

Year	Development
2000 B.C. **Abacus**	The abacus gained popularity fast after it was invented. The later type of abacus was widely used in the Middle East and Asia and is still being used now. Computations are done by sliding beads on a wire arrange on a tray. The term abacus came from the Greek word *abax*, meaning *"flat surface"*.
1617 **Logs and Bones**	John Napier, a Scottish Mathematician, became famous for his invention of logarithms. The use of "logs" reduced a problem of subtraction. In 1617, he invented a computing device using a set of sticks called "bones" which can perform both multiplication and division.
1642 **Arithmetic Engine**	Blaise Pascal, a French Mathematician, invented the "arithmetic engine". The arithmetic engine is the first successful mechanical calculator, which can add and subtract numbers containing up to eight digits.
1670 **Stepped Reckoner**	Gottfried Wilhelm von Leibnitz invented a calculator which can multiply and divide directly, as well as extract square roots. He called it the "stepped reckoner". Again, its drawback was that it was too advanced for the technology at that time.
1800 **Jacquard's Loom**	Joseph Marie Jacquard was the first to successfully use punch cards both for storing information and for controlling the machine. He called it Jacquard's Loom. It became a great commercial success in 1801 and became a milestone in the development of the textile industry and data processing.

1822 **Difference Engine**	An English inventor and mathematician, Charles Babbage, invented the "difference engine." It is a calculator which can compile accurate navigational and artillery tables. Its drawback: it could not also be produced by the technology during that time.
1822 **Analytical Engine**	Babbage also conceived the analytical engine in 1835. The machine has two basic components: memory and mill. The memory or storage unit holds all possible numeric variables and the results of all previous calculations. The "mill" processes data fed to it. The machine has the capacity to compare quantities and then decide which sequence of instructions to follow. The result of processing in the "mill" permits changing of already-stored value. Hence, it has the ability to modify its own program. He described in detail what might have been the world's first working programmable program.
1822 **First Female Programmer**	The assistant of Charles Babbage who helped him in the machine design of his analytic engine was the daughter of the English poet Lord Byron and the Countees of Lovelace, Lady Augusta Ada King. Her understanding of the machine enabled her to create instruction routines that could be fed into the computer. This made her the first female computer programmer. In the 1980's, the U.S. Defense Department named a programming language, **ADA** in her honor.
1827 **Boolean Algebra**	George Boole developed the algebra of logic, which expresses and processes problems in logic by using variables. These variables could only take the value of true or false. The Boolean Algebra, as it was called, became the perfect tool for designing the logic circuits of computers.

1884 **Punched Card Tabulating Machine**	Dr. Herman Hollerith invented the automatic punched card tabulating machine in 1884 and the patent was issued in 1889. Herman Hollerith's machine was the first commercially successful data processing machine. In 1914, he merged his company with two others to form the Computing Tabulating Recording Company, which later, in 1924 became the International Business Machine Corporation, now well known as IBM.
1928 **Cathode Ray Tube (CRT)**	Vladimir Zworykin, a Russian immigrant, invented the Cathode Ray Tube (CRT).
1931 **Z1 Computer**	The designer of the early binary computer was Konrad Zuse. Is work led to a couple of Z Machines (from Z1 to Z4) which eventually led to a series of machines built by the Siemens Corp.
1943 **Colossus**	Allan Turing, a British Mathematician, created a completely electronic computing device called the Colossus. It was a huge version of the ABC, designed to decode German messages. He published an article on Intelligent Machines in 1947. This paper launched the idea of artificial intelligence. It was only in 1956 that John McCarthy coined the acronym AI for Artificial Intelligence.
1945 **1st Computer Bug**	Dr. Grace Murray Hopper, a rear admiral in the United States Navy, was known for her discovery of the first computer bug in the Harvard Mark II computer. She found a moth on the wires of the computer causing it to malfunction, hence the term "bug" and "debugging" originated. The moth or the "bug" now resides in the National Museum of American History in Washington D.C.
1946 **ENIAC**	John Mauchly and J. Presper Eckert from the University of Pennsylvania built the Electronic Numerical Integrator and Calculator (ENIAC). It was the first

	general-purpose electronic computer. The speed of calculation is a thousand times faster than the best mechanical calculator.
1946 **EDVAC**	An improvement of the ENIAC led to the development of Electronic Discrete Variable Automatic Computer (EDVAC). It only used 30% of the vacuum tubes in ENIAC and was much faster in speed. The EDVAC was considered the first stored program computer.
1951 **UNIVAC**	The first commercial computer, Universal Automatic Computer (UNIVAC), was designed by John Mauchly and Presper Eckert. It was successfully in replacing the IBM punched card equipment at the U.S. Bureau of Census using magnetic tape as a buffer memory. In 1953, the first high speed printer was developed by Remington Rand for use in the UNIVAC.
1952 **IBM 701**	IBM introduced the first electronic-stored program computer called 701 which used vacuum tubes and was considered the first-generation computer.
1954 **FORTRAN**	John Backus and his IBM team produced the first successful high-level programming language called Formula Translator (FORTRAN). FORTRAN is often used to create scientific programs on microcomputers and mainframes. The first successful FORTRAN program was run by Harlan Herrick.
1956 **Hard Drive for Machine Computer**	IBM introduced the first hard drive for mainframe called RAMAC 305, which has a total capacity of 5 Mb containing 50 pieces of 24-in. diameter platters.
1958 **Cray Computer**	Seymour Cray built the first fully transistorized supercomputer for Control Data Corporation.
1960 **PDP – 1**	The PDP – 1 (Program Data Processor -) was the first commercial minicomputer equipped with keyboard and monitor. It was introduced by Digital equipment and

	was developed by Benjamin Curley.
1962 **Mouse**	Douglas Engelbart invented the mouse-pointing device for computers.
1964 **BASIC**	The Beginners All Purpose Symbolic Instruction Code (BASIC) programming language was developed by John Kemeny and Thomas Kurtz of Darthmouth.
1964 **Word Processing**	In the same year, IBM coined the term, "Word Processing".
1964 **ASCII**	ASCII (American Standard Code for Information Interchange) was adopted by the American Standard Association as a standard code for data transfer.
1965 **1st Ph. D. in Computer Science**	Richard L. Waxelblat was granted the first Computer Science Ph.D. at the University of Pennsylvania in the same year.
1967 **First Floppy Disk**	The first floppy disk was built by Allan Shugart of IBM. It used an 8-inch plastic disk coated with iron oxide where data could be stored.
1968 **Pascal Programming**	Nicklaus Wirth designed Pascal programming language to help students learn how to program computers. It was purely teaching language which encouraged structures approach to programming.
1972 **C**	Dennis Ritchie and Brian Kernighan developed the C programming language.
1972 **1st Electronic Pocket Calculator**	The first electronic pocket calculator was developed by Jack Kilby, Jerry Merryman and Jim Van Tassel of Texas Instrument.
1973 **CP/M**	Gary Kindall wrote a simple operating system for his Pl/M language and called it CP/M (Control Program/Monitor). He further refined it to fit the Intel 8080-based systems.
1973 **Ethernet**	In November of 1973, Bob Metcalfe of Xerox Palo Alto research Center (PARC) invented the Ethernet computer connectivity system.

COMPUTER EDUCATION 1
ALDRIN DAVE S. QUILINGUIN

1974 **Personal Computer**	Ed Roberts of Micro Instrumentation Telemetry Systems (MITS) began building a small computer based on the Intel 8088 chip. The prototype was completed within the year and was called Altair 8800. He coined the word "personal computer" as a part of the advertising campaign for the Altair. It was considered the first personal computer.
1975 **BASIC**	Bill Gates and Paul Allen from Harvard wrote the first programming language for the Altair, which was called BASIC and licensed it to MITS (Micro Instrumentation Telemetry Systems) in exchange for royalty payment. They later founded Micro-soft and registered it as a company called "Microsoft" in November 1976. Bill Gates dropped out of college after one year to devote his time in managing Microsoft while Paul Allen resigned from MITS and began his full time work at Microsoft in November of 1976.
1976 **Apple 1 Computer**	Steve Wozniak and Steve Jobs finished the computer circuit board of the Apple 1 Computer in 1976. They formed a company called Apple Computer Company on April Full's Day, 1976. While Steve Wozniak designed the Apple computer, Steve Jobs promoted it.
1978 **VisiCalc**	Dan Bricklin, a Harvard Business School student, with the help of Robert Frankston (a computer programmer), and Dan Fylstra (software publisher), developed the first electronic spreadsheet program called VisiCalc. It was released for the Apple computer and became so popular the microcomputer purchase increased just so they could use the software.
1979 **Wordstar**	Robert Barnaby wrote the program Wordstar, which became one of the most popular and bestselling word processors during that time and was released by MicroPro. In relation, GYPSY is one of the

	first word processors termed "WYSIWYG" (what you see is what you get) developed by Xerox PARC in 1975 which runs on the Alto personal computer.
1980 **MS DOS**	IBM chose Microsoft to create an operating system to be used for its soon-to-be launched Personal Computer. Microsoft Disk Operating System (MS DOS) became the standard operating system for computers at that time.
1980 **C++**	Dr. Bjarne Stroustrup of Bell Laboratories created C++ in 10980. It is an object-oriented version of C.
1983 **Lotus 1-2-3**	Lotus 1-2-3 became the spreadsheet software choice for microcomputers, replacing VisiCalc.
1984 **Apple Macintosh**	The Apple Macintosh line was introduced to the computer world as an alternative to the IBM PC. Its operating system has a GUI (Graphical User Interface), which allows users to move screen icons instead of typing instructions. The screen cursor is controlled by a mouse, which mimics the movement of the user's hand on the computer screen.
1985 **Windows**	Microsoft introduced a new kind of operating system. Although it still features DOS commands and functions, Windows has a graphical user interface (GUI), which made it easier for users to operate the computer. Better versions (Windows '95, '98, 2000, XP and others) came out later.
1985 **PageMaker**	Aldus introduced PageMaker for the Macintosh. This started the desktop publishing era. It later introduced in 1987 another version of PageMaker, the IBM PC and Compatibles.
1989 **www**	Timothy Berners-Lee created the technology underlying World Wide Web (www). He proposed a global network of stored documents that would allow physics researchers to access and exchange information.

COMPUTER EDUCATION 1
ALDRIN DAVE S. QUILINGUIN

1994 **Yahoo!**	Jerry Yang and David Filo created the search engine called **Yahoo!**
1994 **OOP**	Ole Johan Dahl and Kristen Nygaard of Norway invented the Object-Oriented Programming, which is the most widely used programming model today. They were awarded the "Nobel Prize of Computing" on February 5, 2002.
1994 **Netscape**	**Marc Andreessen**, with the help of colleagues, developed a program called Mosaic, which allowed the user to move around the web by clicking words and symbols. He formed a company called Netscape Communications Corporation which marketed the Netscape web browser.
1997 **Deep Blue**	Deep Blue, an IBM machine that can make 100 million chess points per second, was able to beat Garry Kasparov, the reigning chess champion in a six-game match in the United States.
2000 **Millennium Bug**	Before the turn of the century, computer experts warned about the possible inability of computer programs to handle the date exchange. Early programmers allowed only two digits to represent the year. The year 200 or Y2K problem caused many users and corporations to prepare. While some problems occurred, no significant difficulties were encountered when the date change happened.
2003 **ASIMO**	Honda Corporation of Japan developed a robot that can walk like a human, go up and down the stairs, greet people and do some simple tasks. This is a breakthrough in artificial intelligence and robotics.

Republic of the Philippines
Nueva Ecija University of Science and Technology
Gabaldon Campus
Gabaldon, Nueva Ecija

LABORATORY HIGH SCHOOL

Name: _____   Score: _____
Grade & Section: _____   Date: _____

TEST I. MULTIPLE CHOICE

> Select the best answer and write it on the space provided before the number.

_____ 1. It is where the data stored permanently.
a. Primary Storage   b. Secondary Storage   c. USB   d. Diskette

_____ 2. The heart and brain of the computer.
a. CPU   b. Hard Disk   c. Monitor   d. Mouse

_____ 3. It consists of devices which communicate the result of processing back to the user.
a. CPU   b. Input Device   c. Output Device   d. Printer

_____ 4. It is a sensitive stylus or pen device that is used by engineers, illustrators and graphic designers.
a. Ball pen   b. Light Pen   c. Status Pen   d. High Pen

_____ 5. A pointing device similar to a mouse but the ball on top is the one directly moved the pointer on the screen.
a. Trackball   b. Mouse   c. Joystick   d. Wheel

_____ 6. It is use for entering characters.
a. Trackball   b. Mouse   c. Joystick   d. Wheel

_____ 7. Skilled person in Information Technology (IT).
a. Peopleware   b. Teacher   c. Computer   d. Librarian

_____ 8. It refers to the physical components of the computer system that you can actually touch.
a. Hardware   b. Software   c. Peopleware   d. Shareware

_____ 9. It is an electronic device which consists of several components that together provide the capability of executing a stored program.
a. Computer   b. Computer System   c. System   d. Elements

_____ 10. It is a device that accepts data, processes and stores these, and produces output.
a. Computer   b. Computer System   c. System   d. Elements

COMPUTER EDUCATION 1
ALDRIN DAVE S. QUILINGUIN

TEST II. IDENTIFICATION

Identify the following and write the answer on the space provided before the number.

_____ 1. It displays images using grids of dots called pixels.
_____ 2. It produces sound output.
_____ 3. Contains data encoded and stored on magnetic stripes.
_____ 4. Kinds of monitor that looks like a traditional TV set.
_____ 5. Translates barcode symbols into digital form.
_____ 6. It captures images in electronic form for immediate viewing on the screen.
_____ 7. It produces hard copy.
_____ 8. It produces soft copy.
_____ 9. Translates images of text, photo and other graphics into digital form.
_____ 10. A pointing device with a base and a vertical handle that pivots in all directions.
_____ 11. Used to output information shown on the screen on a printed paper.
_____ 12. These are the programs used by the user to interact with the computer.
_____ 13. Set of programs and instructions that tell the computer what to do.
_____ 14. A pointing device used to move the cursor on the screen.
_____ 15. It is a display screen that allows user to interact with the system by touching specific areas on the screen.
_____ 16. Who invented the logarithms?
_____ 17. He created the programming language C++.
_____ 18. What do you mean by the acronym ASCII?
_____ 19. A robot that was developed by the Honda Corporation.
_____ 20. Who invented the mouse?

TEST III. ENUMERATION

Enumerate the following.

1-5   Give examples of Input Devices
6-10   Give the limitations of the computer

COMPUTER EDUCATION 1
ALDRIN DAVE S. QUILINGUIN

TEST IV. DRAWING (*10 points*)

Draw and label the Basic Computer Functions

Module 2 - THE WINDOWS DESKTOP

Overview:

Module 1 defines the computer as an electronic digital device that accepts and processes input data and produces resultant information. The computer is a system because it is composed of various parts/devices that work together to serve its purposes.

In this module the students will learn about Windows Desktop. The students will be able to create, move and copy folder and as well as can change the property settings of the computer.

Lesson 1: THE WINDOWS DESKTOP

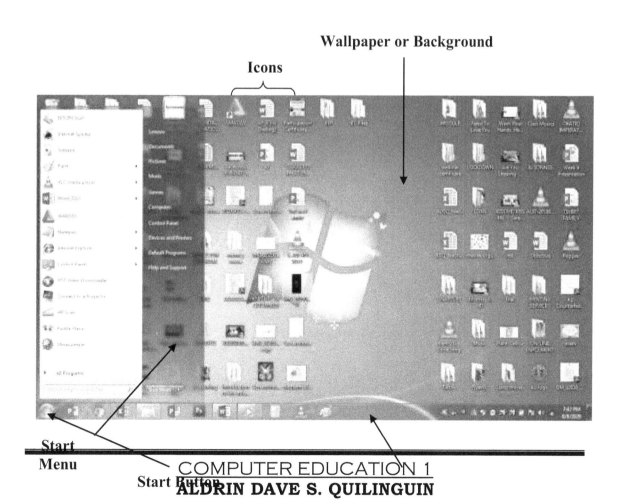

Wallpaper or Background

Icons

Start Menu

Start Button

COMPUTER EDUCATION 1

ALDRIN DAVE S. QUILINGUIN

Win Desktop – is the main interface to a computer system loaded with Win OS. The desktop is the screen itself.

File – is a collection of related records or data in the form of numbers, figures, and characters.

Taskbar – normally appears below the desktop although it may be positioned anywhere by dragging. This bar serves as place for indicating active programs or processes. The taskbar contains the following:

- *Start Button* – appears along the taskbar. In opening a program, you normally click this button to open the start Menu.
- *Start Menu* – provides various options for operating the computer system.

    Among these options are:
- *Programs* – this option opens a sub-menu that displays the Programs loaded in the computer system.
- *Documents* – this options sub-menu of the recently-modified office documents.
- *Settings* – this option is provided for changing the Property Settings of the Computer System.
- *Find* – this is actually a shortcut to the Find program that is used for locating files, folders or computers (if connected to a network).
- *Help* – provides assistance to users having difficulties on working with programs or with the OS environment itself.
- *Run* – provides a dialog box in which you can launch programs by entering its name in the text box provided.
- *Shut Down* – provides a dialog box, the purpose of which is for performing a normal process of turning off the computer system.

Icons – are small graphical images that represent objects like files, folders, programs, devices and shortcuts. A small arrow at the bottom of the icon identifies shortcuts.

The following are the most common desktop icons:

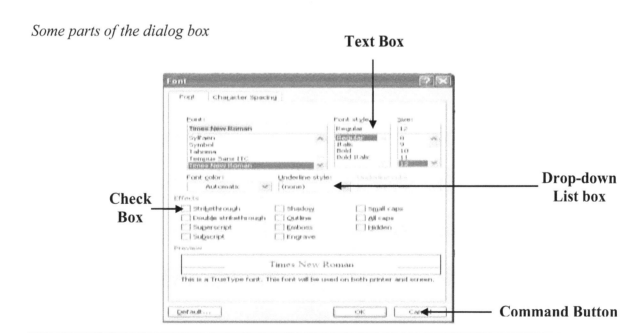

My Computer – provides for the ability to examine or "browse" the components of the computer system by displaying a hierarchical structure of the various parts.

Recycle Bin – this is actually a storage space for files or folders temporarily deleted.

My Documents – the My documents icon is actually a folder that contains your office files created in MS Excel, MS Word and other business application programs.

<u>Shortcuts</u> – are icons on the desktop that serves as quick references to commonly used files and folders or devices.

<u>Dialog boxes</u> – are the main interface between users and programs.

-a window that provides a means of communication between the computer programs and humans/users.

-provides a message or asks for some information.

Some parts of the dialog box

Text Box

Check Box

Drop-down List box

Command Button

COMPUTER EDUCATION 1
ALDRIN DAVE S. QUILINGUIN

❖ *Text box* – a long box where textual data are entered.
❖ *Command button* – these buttons represents commands that are activated when clicked.
❖ *Check box* – enables or disables certain capabilities.
❖ *Drop-down list box* – appears like a text box but contains a down-arrow button at the right.

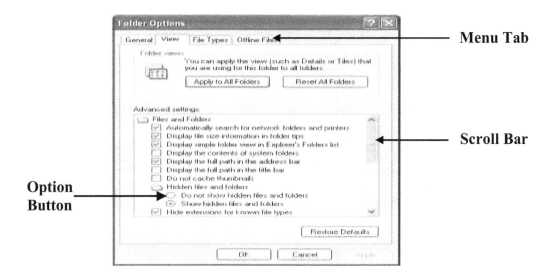

❖ *Option Button* – a group of labeled tiny circles that provides choices.
❖ *Scroll Bar* – there are two scroll bars: Vertical and Horizontal
    - it is used to view/display the remaining contents of a window.

Background or Wallpaper

     – it is another feature in the Graphical User Interface of the Win OS. A computer's background may be personalized by using your chosen picture or image.

Steps in Changing the Background:

1) Right-click the background. A menu appears.
2) Click Properties on the menu. The Displays Properties dialog box appears.
3) On the Menu Tab, click the Desktop.
4) On the list box containing picture files, click the desired background.
5) Click the Display drop-down list box and click Center, Stretch or Tile. Observe how the image changes on the small screen.
6) Click the OK button.
7) If the picture-file you want is not in the list, click Browse button and locate the file by navigating through the file system.

Folders

     – the placeholders of files.

Creating Folders

1) Right click on the Background of the location that you chose. A menu appears, click new, a sub-menu will be displayed and click the word Folder. Rename the folder with something meaningful.
2) On the My Computer, select the hard disk (C:) and on the Task Pane located at the left portion of the screen, click the Make a New Folder on the File and Folder Tasks. Rename the folder with something meaningful.
3) On the My Computer, select the hard disk (C:) and on the Menu Bar, click File and choose New, a sub-menu will be displayed and click the word Folder. Rename the folder with something meaningful.

Copying Files and Folders

1) To copy a file or a folder, simply drag its icon to the target location.
2) Right-click on the file/folder you want to copy and a menu will appear. Choose Copy and select the target location and right-click and click Paste.
3) Select the file/folder you want to copy and click the Copy on the Toolbar. Select the target location and right-click and click paste or click paste on the Toolbar.

4) On the My Computer, select the hard disk (C:) and on the Task Pane located at the left portion of the screen, select the folder and click the Copy this Folder on the File and Folder Tasks. Rename the folder with something meaningful.
5) Select the file/folder you want to copy and on the keyboard, press the shortcut key Ctrl+C *(shortcut key for copy),* select the target location and press the shortcut key Ctrl+V *(shortcut key for paste).*

Moving Files and Folders

1) Right-click on the file/folder you want to move and a menu will appear. Choose Cut and select the target location and right-click and click Paste.
2) Select the file/folder you want to move and click the Cut on the Toolbar. Select the target location and right-click and click paste or click paste on the Toolbar.
3) On the My Computer, select the hard disk (C:) and on the Task Pane located at the left portion of the screen, select the folder and click the Move this Folder on the File and Folder Tasks. Rename the folder with something meaningful.
4) Select the file/folder you want to move and on the keyboard, press the shortcut key Ctrl+X *(shortcut key for cut),* select the target location and press the shortcut key Ctrl+V *(shortcut key for paste).*

Renaming Files and Folders

1) Right-click on the file/folder you want to name. Choose Rename in the menu provided, enter the new name and deselect the object.
2) On the My Computer, select the hard disk (C:) and on the Task Pane located at the left portion of the screen, select the folder and click the Rename this Folder on the File and Folder Tasks. Rename the folder with something meaningful.
3) Select the file/folder you want to rename and on the keyboard, press F2 on the Function Keys, enter the new name and deselect the object.

Republic of the Philippines
Nueva Ecija University of Science and Technology
Gabaldon Campus
Gabaldon, Nueva Ecija

LABORATORY HIGH SCHOOL

Name: _____   Score: _____
Grade & Section: _____   Date: _____

TEST I. MULTIPLE CHOICE

Select the best answer and write it on the space provided before the number.

_____ 1. A group of labeled tiny circles that provides choices.
  a. Option Button   b. Command Button   c. List Box   d. Check Box

_____ 2. It is used to view/display the remaining contents of a window.
  a. Status Bar   b. Command Button   c. Taskbar   d. Scroll Bar

_____ 3. The placeholders of files.
  a. Status Bar   b. Files   c. Folder   d. CPU

_____ 4. Appears like a text box but contains a down-arrow button at the right.
  a. Status Bar   b. Command Button   c. Drop-down list box   d. CPU

_____ 5. Enables or disables certain capabilities.
  a. Option Button   b. Command Button   c. List Box   d. Check Box

_____ 6. These buttons represents commands that are activated when clicked.
  a. Option Button   b. Command Button   c. List Box   d. Check Box

_____ 7. A long box where textual data are entered.
  a. Text box   b. Command Button   c. List Box   d. Check Box

_____ 8. Provides a message or asks for some information.
  a. Dialog box   b. Command Button   c. List Box   d. Check Box

_____ 9. This is actually a storage space for files or folders temporarily deleted
  a. Ricycle Bin   b. Recicle Bin   c. Recycle Ben   d. Recycle Bin

_____ 10. Icons on the desktop that serves as quick references to commonly used files
  and folders or devices.
  a. Icons   b. Shortcuts   c. Iconns   d. Shorcuts

COMPUTER EDUCATION 1
ALDRIN DAVE S. QUILINGUIN

TEST II. IDENTIFICATION

> Identify the following and write the answer on the space provided before the number.

_____ 1. The main interface between users and programs.

_____ 2. A window that provides a means of communication between the computer programs and humans/users.

_____ 3. Provides for the ability to examine or "browse" the components of the computer system by displaying a hierarchical structure of the various parts.

_____ 4. Provides a dialog box, the purpose of which is for performing a normal process of turning off the computer system.

_____ 5. Provides a dialog box in which you can launch programs by entering its name in the text box provided.

_____ 6. Provides assistance to users having difficulties on working with programs or with the OS environment itself.

_____ 7. This is actually a shortcut to the Find program that is used for locating files, folders or computers (if connected to a network).

_____ 8. This option is provided for changing the Property Settings of the Computer System.

_____ 9. This options sub-menu of the recently-modified office documents.

_____ 10. This option opens a sub-menu that displays the Programs loaded in the computer system.

_____ 11. Provides various options for operating the computer system.

_____ 12. Appears along the taskbar. In opening a program, you normally click this button to open the start Menu.

_____ 13. Normally appears below the desktop although it may be positioned anywhere by dragging.

_____ 14. The placeholders of files.

_____ 15. A collection of related records or data in the form of numbers, figures, and characters.

_____ 16. The main interface to a computer system loaded with Win OS. The desktop is the screen itself.

_____ 17. Provides a message or asks for some information.

_____ 18. Enables or disables certain capabilities.

_____ 19. A long box where textual data are entered.

_____ 20. These buttons represents commands that are activated when clicked.

COMPUTER EDUCATION 1
ALDRIN DAVE S. QUILINGUIN

TEST III. ENUMERATION

Enumerate the following.

        1-3   Steps in Renaming Files/Folders
        4-7   Steps in Moving Files/Folders
        8-10   Steps in Creating Files/Folders

TEST IV. DRAWING

Draw and label the Windows Desktop. *(10 points)*

Module 3 - Major Hardware Components of a Computer System

PARTS OF A COMPUTER

PS/2 Mouse – it is a pointing device that used to move the pointer on the screen.

PS/2 Keyboard – use for entering characters.

System Unit – the complete set of computer hardware

AVR – it is a hardware device used to maintain a voltage to electronic devices. It regulates the power.

Power Supply – it converts alternating current to direct current.

Motherboard – it is the main printed circuit board on a computer system.

PARTS OF THE MOTHERBOARD

1.   **Back Panel Connector or Input/output Interface** – it is where the input or output devices are connected.

Motherboard back panel and I/O connectors

⇨ **PS/2 Keyboard Port (violet)** – it is where PS/2 keyboard is connected.

⇨ **PS/2 Mouse Port (green)** – it is where PS/2 mouse is connected.

⇨ **Parallel Port (pink)** – in computing, it is a type of interface found on computers (personal and otherwise) for connecting peripherals. The name refers to the way the data is sent; parallel ports send multiple bits of data at once (parallel communication). It is where the parallel printers and scanners are connected.

➪ **Serial Port (silver)** – in computing, a serial port is a serial communication interface through which information transfers in or out sequentially one bit at a time. It is where the serial mouse is connected.

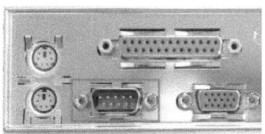 

➪ **VGA Port (blue)** – it is a three-row 15-pin DE-15 connector. The 15-pin VGA connector was provided on many video cards, computer monitors, laptop computers, projectors and high definition television sets. It is where the VGA cable is connected (to monitor).

⇨ **USB Port** – it allows USB devices to be connected to each other with and transfer digital data over USB cables. It is where the USB devices are connected. They can also supply electric power across the cable to devices that need it.

⇨ **Game Port (golden yellow)** – it was originally introduced on the Game Control Adapter, is a device port that was found on IBM PC compatible and other computer systems throughout 1980s and 1990s. it was traditional connector for joystick input and occasionally MIDI devices, until phased out by USB in the late 1990s. It is where the game pad and joysticks are connected.

⇨ **Audio Port (pink, green and blue)** – it is any receptacle or jack to which an audio device suck speakers, headphones or a microphone can be connected. It facilitates the input/output audio signal.

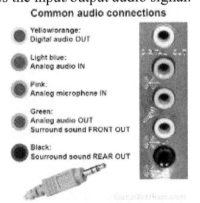 

⇨ **Local Area Network (LAN) Port** – alternatively referred to as Ethernet Port, Network connection and Network Port. The LAN port allows a computer to connect to a network using a wired connection.

2. **4 pin 12 volts connector** – the P4 connector is a 12V power supply cable used in motherboards that have an Intel Pentium 4 or late processors. Today, the connector is a standard power connector and is used with both Intel and AMD motherboards. The P4 cable has two black wires that serve as a ground and two yellow ones that are +12VDC. All of these wires attach to a four pin connection on the motherboard.

 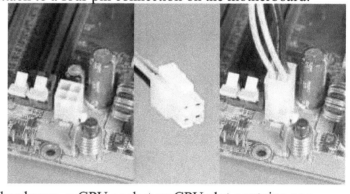

3. **CPU Slot/Socket** – in computer hardware, a CPU socket or CPU slot contains one or more mechanical components providing mechanical and electrical connections between a microprocessor and a printed circuit board (PCB). This allows placing and replacing the CPU without soldering. It holds the CPU.

Kinds:

➪ Pin Grid Array (PGA) type slot

➪ Land Grid Array (LGA) type slot

5. **Memory Card Slot** – it holds the memory card.

6. **Video Card Slot** – it holds the video card.

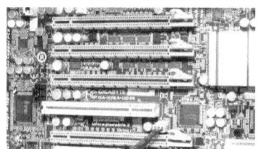 

7. **Expansion Slot or PCI Slot** – it holds expansion cards (Ex. MODEM Card, LAN Card, Sound Card, USB Card).

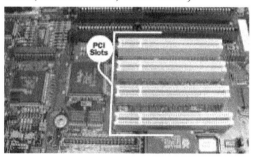 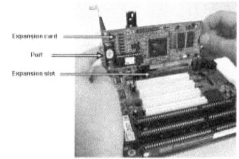

8. **CMOS Slot** – it holds the CMOS battery.

9. **CMOS Battery** – is a chip on the motherboard that contains BIOS configuration, date, time and other information that the computer needs during startup.

10. **BIOS** – it is s firmware used to perform hardware initiation during the booting process (power-on startup), and to provide runtime services for operating systems and programs. It controls the Power on Self-Test (POST).

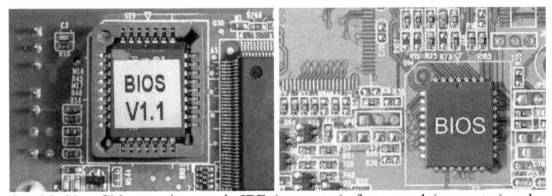

11. **Southbridge Chipset** – it controls IDE (connector), front panel (connector) and back panel (connector). It is also called input and output controller.

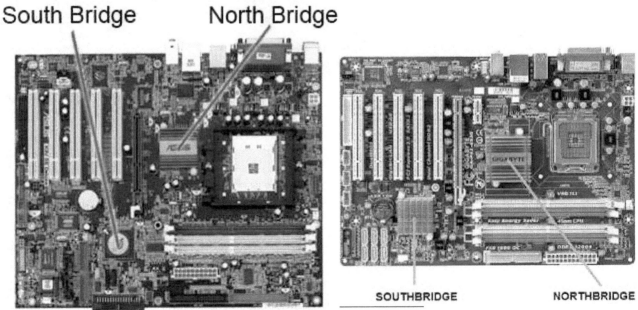

ALDRIN DAVE S. QUILINGUIN

12. **Northbridge Chipset** – it controls memory card and video card. It is also called memory controller.

13. **IDE Connector** – it is where the hard drives and CD/DVD ROM are connected thru an IDE/PATA cable.

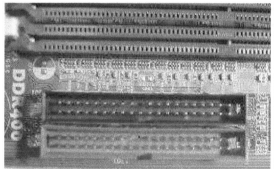 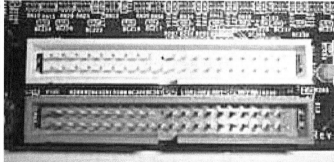

14. **FDD Connector** – where the FDD is connected thru a FDD cable.

 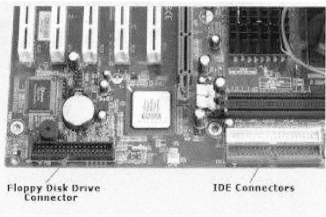

15. **SATA Connector** – it is where SATA devices are connected thru a SATA cable.

16. **Front Panel Connector** – it is where the reset switch, power switch and HDD LED are attached.

17. **Cooling System** – it prevents the CPU from overheating.

Parts:

→ Cooling Fan – it cools the heat sink.

→ Heat Sink – it absorbs heat from the CPU.

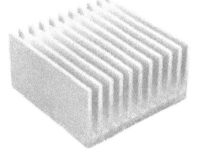

CABLES

1. FDD Cable – it connects the FDD to FDD connector.

2. **VGA Cable** – connects the monitor to VGA port.

3. **IDE Cable or PATA Cable** – connects the IDE devices to IDE connector.

4. **SATA Cable** – it connects SATA devices to SATA connector.

5. **Power Cable** – it connects the power supply to AVR.

1. **Floppy Disk Drive (FDD)** – it reads and writes floppy disks.

2. **Hard Disk Drive (HDD)** – it is the permanent storage of a computer. There are two kinds of HDD; PATA type and SATA type.

3. **CD-ROM and DVD-ROM** – it reads and writes CD-R/DVD-R and CD-RW/DVD-RW.

CARDS

1. **MODEM Card** – it is an internal type of modem that is plugged into the PCI slot of a PC motherboard. It converts analog signal into digital signal.

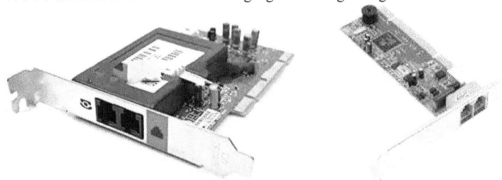

2. **LAN Card** – it is also known as Network Interface Card (NIC). It is used to connect a PC network. The NIC provides a physical connection between the networking cable and the computer's internal bus. It is used for networking.

3. **RAM** – it holds and controls data. The temporary storage of a computer.

4. **Video Card** – it sends video graphical information to the monitor.
   Types:
   a. AGP
   b. PCI-E

PROCESSOR/CPU

1. **LGA (Land Grid Array)** – is a type of surface-mount packaging for integrated circuits that is notable for having the pins on the socket rather than the integrated circuits.

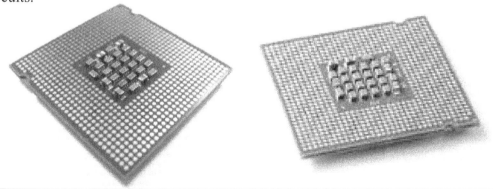

2. **PGA (Pin Grid Array)** – is a connector on a computer's motherboard that accepts a CPU and forms an electrical interface with it.

 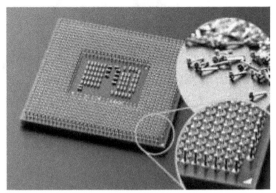

FRONT PANEL

1. **Power Switch** – power on the system unit
2. **Reset Switch** – resets the system unit
3. **Power LED** – the system power LED lights up when system is powered up
4. **HDD LED** – lights up during hard disk activity.

ACRONYMS

1.	AC	-	Alternating Current
2.	AGP	-	Accelerated Graphics Port
3.	ATX	-	Advanced Technology Extended
4.	AVR	-	Automatic Voltage Regulator
5.	BIOS	-	Basic Input Output System
6.	CD	-	Compact Disc
7.	CD-R	-	Compact Disc-Recordable
8.	CD-RW	-	Compact Disc-Rewritable
9.	CMOS	-	Complementary Metal Oxide Semi-conductor
10.	CPU	-	Central Processing Unit
11.	DC	-	Direct Current
12.	DDR-RAM	-	Double Data Rate Random Access Memory
13.	DVD	-	Data Versatile Disc
14.	DVD-R	-	Data Versatile Disc-Recordable

COMPUTER EDUCATION 1
ALDRIN DAVE S. QUILINGUIN

15.	DVD-RW	-	Data Versatile Disc-Rewritable
16.	FDD	-	Floppy Disk Drive
17.	HDD	-	Hard Disk Drive
18.	IDE	-	Integrated Device Electronics
19.	IC	-	Integrated Circuit
20.	ISA	-	Industry Standard Architecture
21.	LAN	-	Local Area Network
22.	LCD	-	Liquid Crystal Display
23.	LED	-	Light Emitting Diode
24.	LGA	-	Land Grid Array
25.	MAN	-	Metropolitan Area Network
26.	MODEM	-	Modulator Demodulator
27.	OHS	-	Occupational Health Safety
28.	PATA	-	Parallel Advanced Technology Attachment
29.	PCB	-	Printed Circuit Board
30.	PCI	-	Peripheral Component Interconnect
31.	PCI-E	-	Peripheral Component Interconnect-Express
32.	PGA	-	Pin Grid Array
33.	POST	-	Power On Self-Test
34.	PS/2	-	Personal System /2
35.	PSU	-	Power Supply Unit
36.	RAM	-	Random Access Memory
37.	ROM	-	Read Only Memory
38.	SATA	-	Serial Advanced Technology Attachment
39.	SDRAM	-	Synchronous Dynamic Random Access Memory
40.	UPS	-	Uninterruptible Power Supply
41.	USB	-	Universal Serial Bus
42.	VGA	-	Video Graphics Accelerator
43.	WAN	-	Wide Area Network

Republic of the Philippines
Nueba Ecija University of Science and Technology
Gabaldon Campus
Gabaldon, Nueva Ecija

LABORATORY HIGH SCHOOL

Name: _____   Score: _____
Grade & Section: _____   Date: _____

TEST I. MULTIPLE CHOICE

Select the best answer and write it on the space provided before the number.

_____ 1. It is an internal type of modem that is plugged into the PCI slot of a PC motherboard.
a. Modem Card   b. LAN Card   c. Video Card   d. RAM

_____ 2. It facilitates input and output audio signals.
a. Speaker   b. Audio Signal   c. Audio port   d. Microphone

_____ 3. The temporary storage of the computer.
a. HDD   b. RAM   c. CPU   d. AVR

_____ 4. It sends video graphical information to the monitor.
a. Video card   b. Audio card   c. Memory card   d. Modem card

_____ 5. It is also known as Network Interface Card (NIC).
a. Modem card   b. LAN Card   c. Video Card   d. RAM

_____ 6. It reads and writes floppy disk.
a. DVD-ROM   b. CD-ROM   c. FDD   d. HDD

_____ 7. It is a chip on the motherboard that contains BIOS configuration, date, time and other information that the computer needs during startup.
a. CMOS battery   b. POST   c. BIOS   d. Motherboard

_____ 8. It is the complete set of computer hardware
a. CPU   b. System unit   c. Mouse   d. Monitor

_____ 9. It is the heart and brain of the computer.
a. HDD   b. RAM   c. Monitor   d. CPU

_____ 10. It holds the Central Processing Unit.
a. Motherboard   b. CPU socket   c. CPU   d. Slot

TEST II. IDENTIFICATION

Identify the following and write the answer on the space provided before the number.

_____ 1. It is a connector on a computer's motherboard that accepts a CPU and forms an electrical interface with it.

_____ 2. It is used to connect a PC network. The NIC provides a physical connection between the networking cable and the computer's internal bus. It is used for networking.

_____ 3. It powers on the system unit.

_____ 4. It is a type of surface-mount packaging for integrated circuits that is notable for having the pins on the socket rather than the integrated circuits.

_____ 5. It is an internal type of modem that is plugged into the PCI slot of a PC motherboard. It converts analog signal into digital signal.

_____ 6. It reads and writes CD-R/DVD-R and CD-RW/DVD-RW.

_____ 7. It is a hardware device used to maintain a voltage to electronic devices.

_____ 8. It is the main printed circuit board on a computer system.

_____ 9. It holds expansion cards (Ex. MODEM Card, LAN Card, Sound Card, USB Card).

_____ 10. In computing, it is a type of interface found on computers (personal and otherwise) for connecting peripherals.

_____ 11. It is alternatively referred to as Ethernet Port, Network connection and Network Port.

_____ 12. It is a chip on the motherboard that contains BIOS configuration, date, time and other information that the computer needs during startup.

_____ 13. It connects the IDE devices to IDE connector.

_____ 14. It connects the power supply to AVR.

_____ 15. It connects SATA devices to SATA connector.

_____ 16. It is where the VGA cable is connected (to monitor).

_____ 17. It is the main printed circuit board on a computer system.

_____ 18. It converts alternating current to direct current.

_____ 19. It is used for entering characters.

_____ 20. It controls the POST.

COMPUTER EDUCATION 1
ALDRIN DAVE S. QUILINGUIN

TEST III. ENUMERATION

Enumerate the following.

1-4   Examples of Cards

5-8   Parts of Front Panel Connector

9-10   Kinds of Processor

Module 4 – Disassemble and Assemble of a System Unit

STEPS TO A SAFE AND SUCCESSFUL DISASSEMBLY AND ASSEMBLY OF A SYSTEM UNIT

TO DISASSEMBLE

1. Prepare all your tools.
   a. Long Philip Screw Driver
   b. Rubber Eraser
   c. Soft Wide Bristle Brush
   d. Paper and Pen for documentation

2. Before opening the system case, be sure to turn off the system unit. Turn off and unplug the AVR from the wall socket as well. After that, unplug all the cables connecting to the back of the system unit. After clearing all the connected cables, put the system unit on an empty working table.

3. Touch the unpainted part of your system unit with your bare hands to remove the ESD of your body. This is an important part before opening your system case. You might destroy your RAM, Chipsets and other components of your motherboard.

4. Remove the screws of the side cover opposite to the side where the ports are. By most system cases, if you are facing the back of the system unit the right side cover is to be removed. Return the screws back to the screw holes to avoid losing them.

5. Once the side cover is removed, turn your system side down where the opened side of the system unit should be facing upward where you can comfortably look down on the inside of your system case.

6. We are now ready to remove the components inside of the computer. The first thing we need to do is remove the power supply. To be able to remove the power supply, remove first the Molex connectors (the white plastic connector at the tip of the wires of the power supply) or the motherboard power connector, drive power connectors, the floppy drive power connector, the SATA power connectors and the four pin 12-volt motherboard connector. With all power connectors are removed from the motherboard and drives, the power supply is now ok to be removed as well. Always have the removed components placed in a remote and safe place away from where you are performing computer disassembly.

7. With the power supply removed, the data cable should be removed next. This includes IDE, SATA, and floppy drive cables. Secure the removed data cables.

8. Next to remove are the RAM, Video Card and other card peripheral components. Again have them secured in a safe place and put the screws back. Clean the connector edges of the card peripherals by rubbing the gold colored edge moderately with a rubber eraser then brushing off the shredding. Do not attempt to clean the edge by blowing or brushing it off with your fingers. Our body is acidic and you might only cause the edges to tarnish faster.

9. Remove all drives. This will include your hard drive, cd/dvd drives, and the floppy drive.

10. Since all peripherals where removed, the next thing to do is to remove the front panel connectors. This will include the USB, Front Panel (FP) and Audio header. If you are not sure of which connector is being match to, write down or document the connections and orientation of the connectors before removing them from the headers. Remember that not all motherboards have the same header configuration so be careful and watchful while documenting.

11. After removing the header connectors, we are now ready to remove the motherboard. To remove the motherboard, locate first all the screws and lightly unscrew all screws alternately. With this technique, we are reducing the risk of warping or bending our motherboard. It may not have a large impact on the bending of the motherboard but still it does have even a little. Upon lightly loosening all screws, remove all screws then. Remove the motherboard by carefully and lightly pulling it away from the I/O shield. Why? Because we need to free the ports that are fitted from the holes in the I/O shield. After freeing the motherboard ports from the I/O shield holes, lift up the motherboard and put it on the safe place.

12. Clean the system unit chassis with your brush, also clean your motherboard and the rest of the peripherals being removed.

TO ASSEMBLE

1. Provided that all peripherals are clean and ready. We are now going to assemble your computer. In assembling back your computer, what we have done during disassembling is just doing the reverse order to assemble it. Since the motherboard was last to be removed, it should then be the first to put back. Remove the retaining screws from the standoff screws of the motherboard and let the motherboard seat on it with the ports facing out towards the I/O shield. Lightly push the motherboard to set

its ports to the holes of the I/O shield. Put the retaining screws on the motherboard screw holes but do not tighten it yet. Now be careful in doing this one and if this is your first time doing it, it is best if you lend a hand for assistance. Lightly push the motherboard towards to I/O shield and lightly tighten the motherboard retaining screws alternately until all screws are tight enough but not too tight. This is to ensure that your ports are protruding correctly out of the I/O shield.

2. Once the motherboard is secured, put back the FP, Audio, and USB header connectors as you will be using your documentation for reference.

3. Put back the drives to the correct drive bays.

4. Connect back the RAM, Video Card and other card peripherals to its proper slot inserting it properly and some cards will require screws to be secured.

5. The data cables (IDE, SATA, floppy cable) should be connected to its proper headers and drives. Remember the proper configuration of the placement of the cables especially if you are dealing with the IDE cables.

6. After the data cables are properly connected, put back the power supply and secure it with the screws you removed earlier. After securing the PSU to the chassis, connect the power connectors to the drives and the motherboard.

7. Once all peripherals are connected properly, have a final inspection by visually checking for loose connection or improper connection. Once the system unit connections are thoroughly checked and verified, connect the keyboard; the monitor, and the power connector then power up the computer. This initial powering up of the computer while the side cover is open ensures us that everything is ok before putting back the side cover. In case something goes wrong, we can accessibly correct the problem right away. If everything is fine shutdown the computer, unplugged the AVR and remove the cables connected to the back of your computer. Put the side cover back.

8. Put the assembled computer back to its place and connect the rest of the cables and connectors. Power it up and see if there are unusual effects of your disassembling/assembling procedure done earlier.

REFERENCES

https://www.computerhope.com/jargon/m/mechmous.htm

https://en.m.wikipedia.org/wiki/Optical_mouse

https://en.m.wikipedia.org/wiki/Liquid-crystal_display

https://www.google.com/amp/s/whatis.techtarget.com/definition/plasma-display%3famp=

https://www.webopedia.com/TERM/I/impact_printer.html

https://www.techopedia.com/definition/6888/dot-matrix-printer-dmp

https://www.webopedia.com/TERM/N/non_impact_printer.html

https://en.m.wikipedia.org/wiki/Inkjet_printing

https://www.google.com/search?q=motherboard++memory+card+slot&tbm=isch&ved=2ahUKEwia0eXnzovrAhVShEsFHWwiCCUQ2-cCegQIABAC&oq=motherboard++memory+card+slot&gs_lcp=ChJtb2JpbGUtZ3dzLXdpei1pbWcQAzoGCAAQBxAeOgQIIxAnOgIIADoECB4QClD8jgFYidwBYNriAWgAcAB4AIAB5gGIAYwTkgEGMC4xMy4xmAEAoAEBwAEB&sclient=mobile-gws-wiz-img&ei=jJsuX5rbEdKIrtoP7MSgqAI&bih=598&biw=360&hl=en&hl=en

https://www.google.com/search?q=ps2+mouse&tbm=isch&ved=2ahUKEwiI_Lb5zovrAhXDHnIKHaFTBuUQ2-cCegQIABAC&oq=ps&gs_lcp=ChJtb2JpbGUtZ3dzLXdpei1pbWcQARgBMgQIIxAnMgQIIxAnMgQIABADMgQIABBDMgQIABBDOgcIIxDqAhAnOgUIABCxA1DJ2gxYttsMYPflDGgCcAB4AIABywGIAfgCkgEFMC4xLjGYAQCgAQGwAQXAAAQE&sclient=mobile-gws-wiz-img&ei=sZsuX8jfEMO9yAOhp5moDg&bih=598&biw=360&hl=en&hl=en#imgrc=CdTMwUx_Lr6m1M

https://www.google.com/search?q=ps2+keyboard&tbm=isch&ved=2ahUKEwjgqsfhz4vrAhUHnEsFHUqQCsAQ2-cCegQIABAC&oq=ps2+&gs_lcp=ChJtb2JpbGUtZ3dzLXdpei1pbWcQARgBMgQIIxAnMgQIIxAnMgQIABBDMgQIABBDMgQIABBDOgIIAFD14AJY6-YCYKbwAmgAcAB4AIABvwGIAcwGkgEDMC41mAEAoAEBwAEB&sclient=mobile-gws-wiz-img&ei=i5wuX6C5J4e4rtoPyqCqgAw&bih=598&biw=360&hl=en&hl=en#imgrc=8K2pqCUvIAVdLM&imgdii=JHMNXErBgADi7M

COMPUTER EDUCATION 1
ALDRIN DAVE S. QUILINGUIN

https://www.google.com/search?q=system+unit&tbm=isch&ved=2ahUKEwiwieb7z4vrA
hXEdysKHdB7CmUQ2-
cCegQIABAC&oq=sy&gs_lcp=ChJtb2JpbGUtZ3dzLXdpei1pbWcQARgAMgQIIxAnM
gQIABBDMgQIABBDMgQIABBDMgQIABBDOgcIIxDqAhAnUNLdAljk3wJgxOkCa
AJwAHgAgAG6AYgB3gKSAQMwLjKYAQCgAQGwAQXAAQE&sclient=mobile-
gws-wiz-
img&ei=wpwuX7CgKcTvrQHQ96moBg&bih=598&biw=360&hl=en&hl=en#imgrc=rL
Y8m1iZVDydiM

https://www.google.com/search?q=avr&tbm=isch&ved=2ahUKEwixnvuV0IvrAhUbHXI
KHSyuBooQ2-
cCegQIABAC&oq=avr&gs_lcp=ChJtb2JpbGUtZ3dzLXdpei1pbWcQARgAMgQIIxAn
MgcIABCxAxBDMgIIADICCAAyAggAOgcIIxDqAhAnOgQIABBDOgUIABCxA1Cm
9wFYlPwBYOKBAmgCcAB4AIABsgGIAfwDkgEDMC4zmAEAoAEBsAEFwAEB&s
client=mobile-gws-wiz-img&ei=-
ZwuX_G9IZu6yAOs3JrQCA&bih=598&biw=360&hl=en&hl=en#imgrc=12zA13lamIH
3YM

https://www.google.com/search?q=power+supply&tbm=isch&ved=2ahUKEwiyqpup0Ivr
AhVTJisKHdNzBE4Q2-
cCegQIABAC&oq=po&gs_lcp=ChJtb2JpbGUtZ3dzLXdpei1pbWcQARgAMgQIIxAnM
gQIIxAnMgQIIxAnMgUIABCxAzIFCAAQsQM6BAgAEEM6BwgjEOoCECdQ664BW
KS5AWDBxAFoAXAAeACAAb0BiAGqBZIBAzAuNJgBAKABAbABAbABBcABAQ&scli
ent=mobile-gws-wiz-
img&ei=IZ0uX_KVONPMrAHT55HwBA&bih=598&biw=360&hl=en&hl=en#imgrc=C
F98skKBA5008M

https://www.google.com/search?q=motherboard&tbm=isch&ved=2ahUKEwiuuJu40IvrA
hVNQH0KHQXLAFgQ2-
cCegQIABAC&oq=m&gs_lcp=ChJtb2JpbGUtZ3dzLXdpei1pbWcQARgCMgQIIxAnM
gQIIxAnMgQIIxAnMgQIABBDMgQIABBDOgcIIxDqAhAnUKbTAVim0wFgjuUBaA
JwAHgAgAHsBIgB7ASSAQM1LTGYAQCgAQGwAQXAAQE&sclient=mobile-gws-
wiz-img&ei=QZ0uX-
6TF82A9QOFloPABQ&bih=598&biw=360&hl=en&hl=en#imgrc=sP1TWWFu7M1vB
M

https://www.google.com/search?q=back+panel&tbm=isch&ved=2ahUKEwiYsKnL0IvrA
hVUcX0KHb0rBIwQ2-
cCegQIABAC&oq=bac&gs_lcp=ChJtb2JpbGUtZ3dzLXdpei1pbWcQARgAMgQIIxAn
MgcIABCxAxBDMgQIABBDMgUIABCxAzIFCAAQsQM6BwgjEOoCECc6BAgAEA
NQlOkBWIjsAWDA-
QFoAnAAeACAAdoBiAHABJIBBTAuMi4xmAEAoAEBsAEFwAEB&sclient=mobile-
gws-wiz-

img&ei=aZ0uX9jXG9Ti9QO915DgCA&bih=598&biw=360&hl=en&hl=en#imgrc=zJw
XfpZQvMrweM

https://www.google.com/search?q=ps2+keyboard+port&tbm=isch&ved=2ahUKEwi8gan
f0IvrAhW-hEsFHZGMAY8Q2-
cCegQIABAC&oq=ps2+key&gs_lcp=ChJtb2JpbGUtZ3dzLXdpei1pbWcQARgCMgQII
xAnMgIIADICCAAyAggAMgIIADoHCCMQ6gIQJzoECAAQQzoECAAQAzoHCAA
QsQMQQ1C51gFYlvwBYPiLAmgCcAB4AIABxAGIAZMJkgEDMC43mAEAoAEBs
AEFwAEB&sclient=mobile-gws-wiz-img&ei=k50uX_zrF76JrtoPkZmG-
Ag&bih=598&biw=360&hl=en&hl=en#imgrc=ueKTWsBz924cpM

https://www.google.com/search?q=parallel+port&tbm=isch&ved=2ahUKEwjl0Zr60IvrA
hWGGrcAHc2nBwsQ2-
cCegQIABAC&oq=parport&gs_lcp=ChJtb2JpbGUtZ3dzLXdpei1pbWcQARgBMgIIAD
IGCAAQBxAeMgYIABAHEB4yBggAEAcQHjIGCAAQBxAeUPmaAljxvQJg0MkCaA
BwAHgAgAHcAYgB8gqSAQUwLjYuMpgBAKABAcABAQ&sclient=mobile-gws-
wiz-img&ei=y50uX6XAL4a13LUPzc-
eWA&bih=598&biw=360&hl=en&hl=en#imgrc=tJTKJN777gBPSM

https://www.google.com/search?q=vga+port&tbm=isch&ved=2ahUKEwiWm9GS0YvrA
hUAGbcAHSJXDNcQ2-
cCegQIABAC&oq=vport&gs_lcp=ChJtb2JpbGUtZ3dzLXdpei1pbWcQARgEMgIIADIC
CAAyAggAMgIIADIGCAAQBxAeOgQIABADOgQIABBDUJzdAVir6AFgtfYBaABw
AHgAgAGoAYgBvwySAQQwLjEwmAEAoAEBwAEB&sclient=mobile-gws-wiz-
img&ei=_50uX9YfgLLctQ-
irrG4DQ&bih=598&biw=360&hl=en&hl=en#imgrc=IHdjBVmzQ6lYaM

https://www.google.com/search?q=usb+port+motherboard+&tbm=isch&ved=2ahUKEwi
vpra50YvrAhVjlrcAHQLCCxkQ2-
cCegQIABAC&bih=598&biw=360&hl=en&hl=en#imgrc=BRxSpxOGLG5pUM

https://www.google.com/search?q=game+port&tbm=isch&ved=2ahUKEwiM_ozB0Yvr
AhUkS3wKHcRqCcoQ2-
cCegQIABAC&oq=ga&gs_lcp=ChJtb2JpbGUtZ3dzLXdpei1pbWcQARgAMgIIxAnM
gQIIxAnMgQIIxAnMgQIABBDMgQIABBDOgcIIxDqAhAnOgQIABADOggIABCxAx
CDAVCS1AFYhtUBYMTdAWgCcAB4AIABpAGIAcMCkgEDMC4ymAEAoAEBsA
EFwAEB&sclient=mobile-gws-wiz-
img&ei=YJ4uX4zOG6SW8QPE1aXQDA&bih=598&biw=360&hl=en&hl=en#imgrc=vs
ErUtx9IixqwM

https://www.google.com/search?q=desktop+audio+port&tbm=isch&hl=en&hl=en&sa=X
&ved=2ahUKEwjJ5-

COMPUTER EDUCATION 1
ALDRIN DAVE S. QUILINGUIN

fi0YvrAhWVTnwKHRQVDAcQrNwCKAB6BQgBEPYB&biw=360&bih=598#imgrc=CKpAj3qCG_4oWM

https://www.google.com/search?q=4+pin+12v+power+connector+slot&tbm=isch&ved=2ahUKEwj_z_7p0YvrAhV-B7cAHThmAAYQ2-cCegQIABAC&oq=4&gs_lcp=ChJtb2JpbGUtZ3dzLXdpei1pbWcQARgAMgQIIxAnMgQIIxAnMgUIABCxAzIFCAAQsQMyAggAOgcIIxDqAhAnUITqAViE6gFgrfgBaAJwAHgAgAGdAYgBnQGSAQMwLjGYAQCgAQGwAQXAAQE&sclient=mobile-gws-wiz-img&ei=tp4uX_-cDP6O3LUPuMyBMA&bih=598&biw=360&hl=en&hl=en#imgrc=LJuI4D2T6JVwfM

https://www.google.com/search?q=pga+slot+type&tbm=isch&ved=2ahUKEwiNis380YvrAhXGGLcAHdW4DRoQ2-cCegQIABAC&oq=pga&gs_lcp=ChJtb2JpbGUtZ3dzLXdpei1pbWcQARgAMgQIIxAnMgQIIxAnMgQIABBDMgQIABBDMgQIABBDOgcIIxDqAhAnUPnDAVj5xwFgvtEBaAJwAHgAgAGYAYgBkwSSAQMwLjOYAQCgAQGwAQXAAQE&sclient=mobile-gws-wiz-img&ei=3Z4uX82nDsax3LUP1fG20AE&bih=598&biw=360&hl=en&hl=en#imgrc=SYfPqxz0t5osQM

https://www.google.com/search?q=lga+slot+type&tbm=isch&ved=2ahUKEwidl6mN0ovrAhUkS3wKHcRqCcoQ2-cCegQIABAC&oq=lga+slot+type&gs_lcp=ChJtb2JpbGUtZ3dzLXdpei1pbWcQA1DtnQFYvp8BYKulAWgAcAB4AIABkwKIAYoEkgEDMi0ymAEAoAEBwAEB&sclient=mobile-gws-wiz-img&ei=AJ8uX52XEqSW8QPE1aXQDA&bih=598&biw=360&hl=en&hl=en#imgrc=NPnsXmqVGzGoAM&imgdii=9DJq_EuGXeWJrM

https://www.google.com/search?q=pga+cpu&tbm=isch&ved=2ahUKEwjhm4Sv0ovrAhX9GbcAHeMCC8kQ2-cCegQIABAC#imgrc=i3LaGgyyII_IVM

https://www.google.com/search?q=lga+cpu&tbm=isch&hl=en&sa=X&ved=2ahUKEwju89Cz0ovrAhUzCLcAHcfpDgkQrNwCKAB6BQgBEPUB&biw=360&bih=598#imgrc=WVh4NPYP8HwmHM

https://www.google.com/search?q=memory+card+slot+motherboard+&tbm=isch&ved=2ahUKEwjF04PY0ovrAhXYELcAHZ1eDuYQ2-cCegQIABAC&oq=memory+card+slot+motherboard+&gs_lcp=ChJtb2JpbGUtZ3dzLXdpei1pbWcQAzoCCAA6BggAEAUQHjoGCAAQCBAeOgQIABAYOgQIHhAKOgQIIRAKUNdLWK-bAWC9oAFoAXAAeACAAAdoFiAHXIJIBDTAuMS40LjEuMi4yLjGYAQCgAQHAAQE&sclient=mobile-gws-wiz-

---

img&ei=nJ8uX8WVO9ih3LUPnb25sA4&bih=598&biw=360&hl=en#imgrc=CH_DlVjC
VifEDM

https://www.google.com/search?q=video+card+slot+on+motherboard&tbm=isch&ved=2
ahUKEwifjMXl0ovrAhWfzHMBHbi-A08Q2-
cCegQIABAC&oq=video+card+slot+motherboard&gs_lcp=ChJtb2JpbGUtZ3dzLXdpei1
pbWcQARgAMgYIABAIEB46BggAEAcQHjoICAAQCBAHEB5Qi8cBWLzZAWCU4
gFoAHAAeACAAYgDiAHDEZIBBzAuMi41LjKYAQCgAQHAAQE&sclient=mobile-
gws-wiz-img&ei=uZ8uX9_LEp-Zz7sPuP2O-AQ&bih=598&biw=360&hl=en#imgrc=8j-
k3wCT7nS5BM

https://www.google.com/search?q=expansion++card+slot+on+motherboard&tbm=isch&
ved=2ahUKEwitiKj60ovrAhWGGrcAHc2nBwsQ2-
cCegQIABAC&oq=expansion++card+slot+on+motherboard&gs_lcp=ChJtb2JpbGUtZ3d
zLXdpei1pbWcQAzoGCAAQBxAeUNf4B1jilQhgmpoIaAFwAHgAgAGaAogB7RGSA
QUwLjcuNJgBAKABAcABAQ&sclient=mobile-gws-wiz-
img&ei=5J8uX62GNYa13LUPzc-eWA&bih=598&biw=360&hl=en#imgrc=H1cezM0-
dqG7BM

https://www.google.com/search?q=cmos+slot&tbm=isch&ved=2ahUKEwii_e6904vrAh
WGPysKHfIzBDcQ2-
cCegQIABAC&oq=cmos&gs_lcp=ChJtb2JpbGUtZ3dzLXdpei1pbWcQARgCMgQIAB
BDMgQIABBDMgQIABBDMgQIABBDMgQIABBDOgcIIxDqAhAnOgQIIxAnOgQI
ABADUOvbBFit4ARg2uoEaAJwAHgAgAG2AYgBuAWSAQMwLjSYAQCgAQGwA
QXAAQE&sclient=mobile-gws-wiz-
img&ei=cqAuX6L8IIb_rAHy55C4Aw&bih=598&biw=360&hl=en#imgrc=RVM8GjhIr
1_vXM

https://www.google.com/search?q=bios+hardware&tbm=isch&hl=en&hl=en&sa=X&ved
=2ahUKEwjHtvGw1IvrAhWRGCsKHRu3AxcQrNwCKAJ6BQgBEO0B&biw=360&bi
h=598#imgrc=LkOIP8l1sAPeCM

https://www.google.com/search?q=southbridge+chipset&tbm=isch&ved=2ahUKEwiwra
W21IvrAhVdkksFHQXqCP0Q2-
cCegQIABAC&oq&gs_lcp=ChJtb2JpbGUtZ3dzLXdpei1pbWcQARgAMgcIIxDqAhAn
MgcIIxDqAhAnMgcIIxDqAhAnMgcIIxDqAhAnMgcIIxDqAhAnUABYAGDEEmgCcA
B4AIABAIgBAJIBAJgBAKABAbABBcABAQ&sclient=mobile-gws-wiz-
img&ei=b6EuX_C5Bd2krtoPhdSj6A8&bih=598&biw=360&hl=en&hl=en#imgrc=-
0cv4OqUphmZKM&imgdii=2EDpIbz4occtXM

https://www.google.com/search?q=ide+slot&tbm=isch&hl=en&hl=en&sa=X&ved=2ahU
KEwjPperv1YvrAhWSAbcAHfIvBRYQrNwCKAB6BQgBEK0B&biw=360&bih=598#i
mgrc=KrjA0MMg9lTeHM

---

https://www.google.com/search?q=fdd+slot+motherboard&tbm=isch&ved=2ahUKEwjC kI_21YvrAhXI0XMBHRkGAwoQ2-cCegQIABAC&oq=fdd+slot&gs_lcp=ChJtb2JpbGUtZ3dzLXdpei1pbWcQARgBMgIIA DIECAAQGDoGCAAQBxAeOgQIIxAnOgQIABBDOgUIABCxA1C7qAVY-rcFYOXEBWgAcAB4AIABsgGIAbkHkgEDMC42mAEAoAEBwAEB&sclient=mobile-gws-wiz-img&ei=AaMuX4KMF8ijz7sPmYyMUA&bih=598&biw=360&hl=en&hl=en#imgrc=A HFqM5C8CLPzTM

https://www.google.com/search?q=front+panel+connectors&tbm=isch&ved=2ahUKEwj y-7Ok1ovrAhWPGbcAHeEADMAQ2-cCegQIABAC&oq=front&gs_lcp=ChJtb2JpbGUtZ3dzLXdpei1pbWcQARgCMgQIABB DMgQIABBDMgQIABBDMgQIABBDMgIIADoHCCMQ6gIQJzoECCMQJzoECAAQ AzoFCAAQsQNQxtEHWKvYB2Du5wdoAnAAeACAAawBiAHABpIBAzAuNZgBAK ABABbABBcABAQ&sclient=mobile-gws-wiz-img&ei=YqMuX_LCG4-z3LUP4YGwgAw&bih=598&biw=360&hl=en&hl=en#imgrc=scL8FCczT84kKM

https://www.google.com/search?q=cooling+system+motherboard+&tbm=isch&ved=2ah UKEwiv0sui14vrAhVY0nMBHa3oC3cQ2-cCegQIABAC&oq=cooling+system+motherboard+&gs_lcp=ChJtb2JpbGUtZ3dzLXdpei 1pbWcQAzIGCAAQCBAeOgQIABBDOgIIADoHCCMQBRAeUN8MWORhYIpoaAB wAHgAgAGbBogB9BmmSAQ0wLjYuMC4xLjAuMi4xmAEAoAEBwAEB&sclient=mo bile-gws-wiz-img&ei=a6QuX-_wBNikz7sPrdGvuAc&bih=598&biw=360&hl=en&hl=en#imgrc=ZP82BA5q7UKw0M

https://www.google.com/search?q=cooling+fan&tbm=isch&ved=2ahUKEwijzIes14vrAh XD2HMBHUwWAakQ2-cCegQIABAC&oq=cooling+&gs_lcp=ChJtb2JpbGUtZ3dzLXdpei1pbWcQARgCMgQII xAnMgQIIxAnMgQIABBDMgQIABBDMgQIABBDOgcIIxDqAhAnOgQIABADUOff BljT8AZgoPYGaAJwAHgAgAHaAYgB_wmSAQUwLjcuMZgBAKABABbABBcABAQ &sclient=mobile-gws-wiz-img&ei=fqQuX6OVOcOxz7sPzKyEyAo&bih=598&biw=360&hl=en&hl=en#imgrc=PD L2tv7rSrJ_3M

https://www.google.com/search?q=heat+sink&tbm=isch&ved=2ahUKEwjbiozo14vrAhX DHnIKHaFTBuUQ2-cCegQIABAC&oq=heat&gs_lcp=ChJtb2JpbGUtZ3dzLXdpei1pbWcQARgBMgIIABB DMgQIABBDMgQIABBDMgQIABBDMgQIABBDOgcIIxDqAhAnOgQIIxAnOgQIA BADUPnUAljP2QJg7OACaAJwAHgAgAGzAYgBggWSAQMwLjSYAQCgAQGwAQ XAAQE&sclient=mobile-gws-wiz-img&ei=_KQuX9ucM8O9yAOhp5moDg&bih=598&biw=360&hl=en&hl=en#imgrc=L Ko975UtK2SuDM

https://www.google.com/search?q=fdd+cable&tbm=isch&ved=2ahUKEwjs_r2A2IvrAh
UBkksFHc0DCJAQ2-
cCegQIABAC&oq=fdd+ca&gs_lcp=ChJtb2JpbGUtZ3dzLXdpei1pbWcQARgAMgIIAD
ICCAAyAggAMgYIABAIEB4yBggAEAgQHjoHCCMQ6gIQJzoECCMQJzoECAAQA
zoECAAQQ1DVlQNY2KgDYOKzA2gCcAB4AIABtwGIAaQHkgEDMC42mAEAoAE
BsAEFwAEB&sclient=mobile-gws-wiz-
img&ei=L6UuX6yrPIGkrtoPzYeggAk&bih=598&biw=360&hl=en&hl=en#imgrc=FeyT
J9wd0p2JSM

https://www.google.com/search?q=vga+cable&tbm=isch&ved=2ahUKEwiK86qf2IvrAh
VDbisKHdNmBbcQ2-
cCegQIABAC&oq=vga+cable&gs_lcp=ChJtb2JpbGUtZ3dzLXdpei1pbWcQAzIECAAQ
QzIECAAQQzIECAAQQzICCAAyAggAOgcIIxCwAhAnOgQIABANOgYIABAHEB4
6BwgAELEDEEM6BQgAELEDULzmAlihgwNgsY4DaABwAHgAgAHEAYgBngqSA
QMwLji YAQCgAQHAAQE&sclient=mobile-gws-wiz-
img&ei=cKUuX4r7KcPcrQHTzZW4Cw&bih=598&biw=360&hl=en&hl=en#imgrc=k4q
XJ1kYRpoaLM

https://www.google.com/search?q=sata+cable&tbm=isch&ved=2ahUKEwjQ-
6O92IvrAhWLeH0KHUisAAcQ2-
cCegQIABAC&oq=sata&gs_lcp=ChJtb2JpbGUtZ3dzLXdpei1pbWcQARgAMgIIABB
DMgQIABBDMgQIABBDMgQIABBDMgQIABBDOgcIIxDqAhAnOgQIIxAnOgQIA
BADUKPQBFiT1ARgr94EaAJwAHgAgAGRAogBqQaSAQUwLjMuMZgBAKABAb
ABBcABAQ&sclient=mobile-gws-wiz-
img&ei=r6UuX5DoHYvx9QPI2II4&bih=598&biw=360&hl=en&hl=en#imgrc=78NK2n
ApI4D3sM&imgdii=FV0RJXHZJ9tTeM

https://www.quora.com/Where-is-the-SATA-cable-connector-in-a-motherboard

https://www.google.com/search?q=power+cable&tbm=isch&ved=2ahUKEwi2gufg2Yvr
AhUbk0sFHaRQBXAQ2-
cCegQIABAC&oq=power+cable&gs_lcp=ChJtb2JpbGUtZ3dzLXdpei1pbWcQAzICCA
AyAggAMgIIADICCAAyAggAOgcIABCxAxBDOgUIABCxAzoGCAAQBxAeOgQIA
BANUPyXBliFugZgnMAGaABwAHgAgAHiAYgBxA2SAQUwLjguMpgBAKABAcA
BAQ&sclient=mobile-gws-wiz-img&ei=BqcuX7bnGZumrtoPpKGVgAc&client=ms-
android-oppo&prmd=isvn#imgrc=kP4xteceg3HEJM

https://www.google.com/search?q=fdd&tbm=isch&hl=en&chips=q:fdd,g_1:computer:L
AxnR0ZDrfc%3D&client=ms-android-
oppo&prmd=isvn&hl=en&sa=X&ved=2ahUKEwiS7pPA2ovrAhW8kEsFHTO7C1oQ4l
YoAnoECAEQDg&biw=360&bih=598#imgrc=STmaYe8trNORpM

https://www.google.com/search?q=hdd+sata&tbm=isch&ved=2ahUKEwj6_6SZ24vrAh
XQSSsKHbUYCVAQ2-
cCegQIABAC&oq=hdd+sata&gs_lcp=ChJtb2JpbGUtZ3dzLXdpei1pbWcQARgAMgQI
ABBDMgIIADICCAAyAggAMgIIAFCoqQFYra8BYPS6AWgAcAB4AIAB-
ASIAbcTkgEFNC00LjGYAQCgAQHAAQE&sclient=mobile-gws-wiz-
img&ei=iaguX7qXE9CTrQG1saSABQ&bih=598&biw=360&client=ms-android-
oppo&prmd=isvn&hl=en&hl=en#imgrc=gQUJkKeCHRgzDM

https://www.google.com/search?q=cd+rom&tbm=isch&hl=en&chips=q:cd+rom,g_1:driv
e:0plBS8se3_Y%3D&client=ms-android-
oppo&prmd=isvn&hl=en&sa=X&ved=2ahUKEwiNtN3A3IvrAhWBhEsFHdrOAlMQ4l
YoAnoECAEQDg&biw=360&bih=598#imgrc=3Iz3EUilRo8ktM

https://www.google.com/search?q=modem+card&tbm=isch&ved=2ahUKEwi0rpuE3Yvr
AhXCm0sFHTI2BS8Q2-
cCegQIABAC&oq=modem+ca&gs_lcp=ChJtb2JpbGUtZ3dzLXdpei1pbWcQARgDMgII
ADICCAAyAggAMgIIADICCAA6BwgjEOoCECc6BAgjECc6BAgAEEM6BwgAELE
DEEM6BQgAELEDUNDtBVjsiQZgoZYGaAJwAHgAgAG7AYgBjQqSAQMwLjiYA
QCgAQGwAQXAAQE&sclient=mobile-gws-wiz-img&ei=daouX_SfPMK3rtoPsuyU-
AI&bih=598&biw=360&client=ms-android-
oppo&prmd=isvn&hl=en&hl=en#imgrc=lhlAKAYk9BwlCM

https://www.google.com/search?q=lan+card&tbm=isch&ved=2ahUKEwjCvK3l3YvrAh
Wj23MBHQzwCasQ2-
cCegQIABAC&oq=&gs_lcp=ChJtb2JpbGUtZ3dzLXdpei1pbWcQARgBMgcIIxDqAhAn
MgcIIxDqAhAnMgcIIxDqAhAnMgcIIxDqAhAnMgcIIxDqAhAnUABYAGDAiANoAn
AAeACAAQCIAQCSAQCYAQCgAQGwAQXAAQE&sclient=mobile-gws-wiz-
img&ei=QasuX4KYK6O3z7sPjOCn2Ao&bih=598&biw=360&client=ms-android-
oppo&prmd=isvn&hl=en&hl=en#imgrc=YWbV6GQ_t1lm6M

https://www.google.com/search?q=memory+card+computer&tbm=isch&ved=2ahUKEwj
juMP93ovrAhXCYH0KHaDnCxkQ2-
cCegQIABAC&oq=memory+card+com&gs_lcp=ChJtb2JpbGUtZ3dzLXdpei1pbWcQA
RgAMgIIADICCAAyAggAMgIIADICCAA6BAgjECc6BAgAEENQB1juUWCxX2gAc
AB4AIABlAWIAcgQkgEHMy0xLjEuMpgBAKABAcABAQ&sclient=mobile-gws-wiz-
img&ei=gKwuX-P4MsLB9QOgz6_IAQ&bih=598&biw=360&client=ms-android-
oppo&prmd=isvn&hl=en&hl=en#imgrc=qrF1ht2Yi-GITM

https://www.google.com/search?q=video+card+computer&tbm=isch&ved=2ahUKEwjPh
4GG34vrAhVbkksFHYMEClIQ2-
cCegQIABAC&oq=vide+card+computer&gs_lcp=ChJtb2JpbGUtZ3dzLXdpei1pbWcQA
RgAMgQIABANMggIABAIEAcQHjIICAAQCBAHEB4yCAgAEAgQBxAeMggIABA
IEAcQHjoCCAA6BggAEAcQHlD1igRYi50EYMujBGgAcAB4AIABxQGIAZ0NkgEE

MC4xMJgBAKABAcABAQ&sclient=mobile-gws-wiz-img&ei=kqwuX8_2JdukrtoPg4mokAU&bih=598&biw=360&client=ms-android-oppo&prmd=isvn&hl=en&hl=en#imgrc=cIkPWytWKux_aM&imgdii=ACKVTw5ROHCiTM

https://en.m.wikipedia.org/wiki/Serial_port

https://en.m.wikipedia.org/wiki/Parallel_port

https://en.m.wikipedia.org/wiki/VGA_connector

https://www.lifewire.com/what-is-a-usb-port-818166

https://www.lifewire.com/what-is-a-usb-port-818166

https://itstillworks.com/audio-port-computer-18204.html

https://www.computerhope.com/jargon/p/p4.htm

https://www.google.com/search?q=24+pin+atx+slot&tbm=isch&ved=2ahUKEwiurNab8IvrAhUYArcAHQnCDf4Q2-cCegQIABAC&oq=24+pin+atx+sloy&gs_lcp=ChJtb2JpbGUtZ3dzLXdpei1pbWcQARgAMgQIHhAKOgQIABBDOgYIABAIEB46BAgAEBg6AggAUJIOWItLYP9VaAJwAHgAgAGrAYgBpAiSAQMwLjeYAQCgAQHAAQE&sclient=mobile-gws-wiz-img&ei=k74uX-6WHJiE3LUPiYS38A8&bih=598&biw=360&client=ms-android-oppo&prmd=isvn&hl=en#imgrc=YLwpChtIB3xUgM

https://en.m.wikipedia.org/wiki/CPU_socket

https://www.quora.com/What-is-a-CMOS-battery-What-are-its-functions

https://en.m.wikipedia.org/wiki/BIOS

https://www.google.com/search?q=ide+cable&client=ms-android-oppo&hl=en&prmd=isvn&sxsrf=ALeKk02IGyG5BBCsCzQmhuS6vAgp3oonOQ:1596902153934&source=lnms&tbm=isch&sa=X&ved=2ahUKEwjz24CN_IvrAhXRgeYKHTdECCUQ_AUoAXoECBIQAQ&biw=360&bih=598#imgrc=XFMmlzGaDcpHlM&imgdii=P6BqwmiCW1tnuM

https://www.techopedia.com/definition/25901/modem-card

https://www.quora.com/What-is-LAN-card

https://www.google.com/search?client=ms-android-oppo&hl=en&sxsrf=ALeKk033pLt5i9dZPqc2YqWp5c52K4o39Q:1596903655112&q=lan+port&tbm=isch&chips=q:lan+port,g_1:computer:qu0cHmHyY_0%3D&usg=AI4_-kSpg5AUgOVd-c0EpTUwewN0RSxcjQ&sa=X&ved=2ahUKEwiQzenYgYzrAhXKXSsKHSpMD6YQgIoDKAB6BAgEEAM&biw=360&bih=598#imgrc=_VcIyR1lQC2p1M